Five Steps to the Perfect Pet

Mike Deathe CPDT-KA

Published by FastPencil Publishing

Five Steps to the Perfect Pet

First Edition

Print edition ISBN: 9781619330450

Copyright ©

Sale of this book without a front cover may be unauthorized. If the book is coverless, it may have been reported to the publisher as "unsold or destroyed" and neither the author nor the publisher may have received payment for it.

http://www.fastpencil.com

Printed in the United States of America

Table of Contents

Why write this book? 13

This is not an obedience book 17

I don't care how you do it . . . I just care if you know why you are doing it. 19

Why does my dog do that? 23

Resource Control Vs. Dominance Control or Parent vs. Butt-Head 25

Hand Feeding 29

Sit Say Please...33

Non-Negotiable Rules 39

Problem Behaviors and The 15 Minute Ignore ...45

Exercise: Reality Vs. Myth 51

Will This Stuff Really Work? 59

Its been a difficult year and this book has been my catharsis I only hope it helps folks with their dogs as it did me getting through a tough time... I know I am gonna forget someone but here it goes... Pat and Rene for all the support My Mom and My Sister for all the late night talks Donovan and Dylan for just being you Kate for the memories And all the dogs who I have had the pleasure from learning from! Mike

To every dog, dog trainer and client I have had a pleasure to know because if it were not for you this book would not be possible.

Okay, so here I sit at the keyboard again. Except this time, it's the third book . . .

This is a book I've wanted to write for several years now. Five Easy Steps to a Perfect Pet Dog — what a name! If I had not been teaching these five basic ideas to my clients for the last three years, that title might just scare me a little. But I've seen over and over how these ideas change not only dogs, but also their owners.

A word of caution though: if you're not consistent, if you do not practice or if you place this book under your pillow while waiting for osmosis to kick in, these ideas will not work!

However, if you work with your dog a few times each day for about 15 minutes, get everyone in the family on the same page and are consistent with rules and routines, then you are definitely on your way to a perfect pet dog! I guarantee these ideas will work on your dog. But what I cannot guarantee is that they will work on you . . . so go in with eyes wide open. Be ready to put in the work and the time and, I promise, good things will come back to you!

So, a little about me. My name is Mike Deathe and I'm a certified dog trainer CPDT-KA from Shawnee, Kansas. I have been training dogs since 2008 and I own a business called Keep it Simple Stupid (KISS) Dog Training. Also, I am an evaluator for the AKC's Canine Good Citizen Certification. This is my third book, and I've contributed articles to magazines around the country. I even started working with a new pet website this year as an online "resident expert." I don't say any of this to make myself sound more important, but some folks like to know about a person's credentials, so now you have them.

How about we both agree for me to keep writing and you to keep reading – and we'll leave whether this book was worthwhile or not until the end? A favor though: if you do like the book, please give me an honest review on Amazon, iTunes or some other online bookstore. Small authors like myself need all the help we can get!

So now you know a little bit about the book and a little bit about me. Let's get into the meat and potatoes of the book with Chapter 1: Why Write This Book?

– Mike

Why write this book?

If there is one truth in dog training, it's this: there is no one way to train a dog! Now, I'm warning you up front because there are a ton of trainers out there who would have you believe the exact opposite. In other words, these trainers would say their way is the only way to train a dog. But believe me when I say it – I am not now, nor will I ever be, the smartest dog trainer out there. My ideas are not really even all that original.

Trust me, I started by reading books by Ian Dunbar, Nicholas Dodman, Paul Owens . . . the list goes on. My ideas build from theirs, just as their ideas did from others. I simply took ideas I liked, used them and let those ideas evolve into the topics we'll cover in this book. Does that mean you are going to like everything you read? I doubt it. To be honest, I hope you cuss, discuss and chew on every idea you find in this book. Because without thoughts and opinions, nothing will ever change.

Over the past several years, I found there were five articles from my blog that became more and more popular. These five got more views, comments and results than many other articles I penned. In fact, my first session with clients often focused on these five topics as a way to jump-start training and leadership and to help with owner frustration. I even started carrying copies of these articles in my car to give to each client after our session, so they had something to refer to after I left. Then, one day, a client made two comments that have stuck with me, and been repeated by others a few times as well:

1. You know, everything you just taught me is really nothing more than common sense and I really should have been able to figure this out on my own . . .

2. Why on earth have you not put these ideas into a book, you fool!

Well, that was about three years ago. During that time, we finished up our book on potty training - that's *The Dog Owner's Book of Poop and Pee* - and then also released a book for shelter volunteers called *Forever Home . . . Dog Training 101 & How to be a Better Shelter Volunteer* . And now that both are done, I sit here with my outline in hand and begin *Five Easy Steps to a Perfect Dog* .

I promise you nothing but a fun book about how you and your pooch can learn to speak the same language and how you can achieve that elusive goal of a great "pet dog." Let's move on to one of my main differences with other dog trainers. I do not like being called an obedience trainer; rather, I prefer to be called a Pet Dog Trainer.

This is not an Obedience Book

From my perspective, being an obedience dog trainer is boring! I could care less that my dog can do a three minute sit and stay with a back flip off the high dive . . . I would rather have a calm dog within the four walls of my home, a dog who can go out in public with me without losing my mind. This, my friend, is what I call a Pet Dog and what I want to be known for training.

So if you do competition obedience, agility or some other form of competition with your dog, this might not be the perfect book for you (but I still bet you'll get something out of it). If you are, on the other hand, someone frustrated that:

1. **Your dog does not listen or pay attention**
2. **Your dog has absolutely no impulse control**
3. **Your dog is too rough, out of control and treats you like another dog to be played with**
4. **Your dog has no concept of how to live with a family of humans**

Well, I think you just bought the right book . . .

We are going to teach the skills necessary to create the perfect pet dog, not an obedience champion. So if this sounds like a plan you can get behind, keep flipping pages.

Now, the next thing we need to get straight: which of the following two statements is more important?

- ***I need to know how to train my dog step by step***

Or

- ***I need to know why my dog is behaving the way he or she is***

Well, what do you think?

I DON'T CARE HOW YOU DO IT . . . I JUST CARE IF YOU KNOW WHY YOU ARE DOING IT.

Okay, let me be clear: you are the one with the big frontal lobe. You are the one with all that grey matter and opposable thumbs to boot. So don't be shocked when I tell you I could care less how you train your dog. Each client I have had over the years has done it differently. That, my friends, is what makes us human. And, to be honest, it would drive me nuts to have a dog trainer tell me it's important to stand with my weight on my left foot, while I hold the treat in my right hand and say the command with a particular pitch and tone . . .

Sure, there are tricks we dog trainers know, tricks like which hand to hold the treat in, and, yes, we will tell you that tone and pitch are important. But I hate to break it to you, these are all secondary to understanding why your pooch has been engaging in a particular behavior! Without understanding why a behavior is happening, how on God's green earth are we supposed to figure out what to do to fix it?

Well, in many cases, we resort to yelling, screaming and punishing. That's being reactive, not proactive. But what if I told you much of the research coming out today says dogs (adult dogs, no less) have the intelligence level of a pre-verbal toddler -- let's say that of a two or three year old! Wouldn't that change the way you look at and react to your dog?

Well, folks, this brings us to one of the biggest differences between me and some other trainers out there . . . I don't train dogs. I train owners! If I can teach you why Fido is doing what he is doing, then I damn sure can teach you how get him to do something else. My goal with this book is not only to teach you why dogs engage in some really irritating-to-us behaviors, but also what we can do to get back to ground zero and replace bad behaviors with good behavior.

Trust me: once you understand the "whys" of dog training, I bet you can come up with your own "how to." Don't worry, we are going to cover those as well! Just understand that, in my humble opinion, the important part of this book is to first understand the problems. Then, and only then, can we try to fix the behaviors you see in your dog.

So let's get right down the nitty gritty, as they say, and ask an important question: **why does Fido do that?**

Why does my dog do that?

The eternal question of dog training: **why does my dog do that?**

Now, to be honest, I could care less what *that* is, because it does not matter! Yep, I said it! All problem behaviors are based on the same simple idea: your dog does *fill-in-the-blank* because it works! No highbrow, complicated or in-depth reason. Just because the behavior works, plain and simple.

Think about it. Why does Fido pull on the leash? Because it works. It gets him from Point A to Point B. He has figured out the fastest way to get what he wants -- to just drag you along for the ride . . .

Ask yourself: what would Fido do if you stopped walking and just stood there every time he pulled on the leash? After all, what does Fido really want? Well, Fido wants to continue his walk. Trust me, if your dog knew the walk stopped every time the leash was tight, there would be no reason to pull. Not sure? Let's look at another example . . .

How about the one where Fido plays too rough, he jumps up and is too rough with his mouth when he is playing? Those teeth hurt and might even leave bruises! Well, folks, Fido is playing with you like he would play with another dog. Dogs play rough and, unfortunately, no one has ever taught him there are separate rules for playing with humans!

What, you ask, is Fido getting out of all this rough play? It's simply your attention. As long as you allow him to continue the play, there is no reason for him to stop. Now I won't tell you, as some trainers might, that you need to forcibly make him stop the rough play. Rather, we need Fido to lose access to the one thing he really wants -- and that's you! I want Fido to understand that rough or inappropriate play will make the one thing he wants more than anything -- you -- go away.

Just like with kids, there is a consequence to every action. And once Fido figures this out, you are well on your way to training your dog! Just what are the specifics of teaching this kind of control and leadership? Well, I like to call it training via resource control!

Resource Control vs. Dominance Control or Parent vs. Butt-Head

As I hinted in the last chapter, there are two basic ways to train a dog:

  _ **1. Dominance Control Training –** _ _ **You will do what I say because I say so.** _

  _ **2. Resource Control Training –** _ * *You will do what I say because the only way you get what you want is when I get what I want.* *

In a matter of speaking, dog training is more like playing hard to get, rather than forcing into submission. Let's face it: in most cases, what your dog really wants is you or your attention. And so he simply does things that get you to react, things that get you to give him what he wants. Really, it is the dog training the owner in most cases.

However, consider what would happen if you, the person (remember – grey matter, thumbs, etc.), were to start controlling access to all the things Fido enjoys. If you made him start working for those things, it would not take long for your dog to shift his thinking. Looking at the world through the prism of "What makes my master happy?" would make sure Fido always gets what he wants. Fido would start to see that, by simply making sure his owner gets what he or she wants first, he would get more of what makes him happy!

The simple question is this: would you rather be a butt-head to your dog and get the behavior you want via threat of punishment, or teach your dog that all the stuff of value to him comes through you? Wouldn't you rather teach Fido that through rules and routines he will gain access to all the things he wants in life?

Resource control training is what this book is really all about. I have found four ways to teach the techniques to your dog. And, trust me, they live up to the name of my business – "Keep it Simple Stupid" Dog Training. Then, of course, the fifth tip is a bonus we just throw in because it works so well.

_ **So the five topics are:** _
_ 1.   **Hand Feeding** _
_ 2.   **Sit Say Please** _
_ 3.   **Non Negotiable Rules** _
_ 4.   **Problem Behaviors and the 15 Minute Ignore** _

_ 5. **Exercise and how it affects behavior – also known as, "A Tired Dog is a Good Dog." _**

So, that is it, folks! The next five chapters will delve into each topic in detail and will go over some ways to accomplish each. It really is that easy. But, that being said, I must remind you: while these topics are not hard to understand, they do require consistency and frequency in order to work. So if you don't plan on putting in some pretty serious time with your dog . . . well, no amount of reading or dog training books will help you! But enough of the negative stuff. Let's get to the reason you bought this book: the five steps to a perfect dog!

Hand Feeding

I always get one particular question from folks when they find out I am a dog trainer: "What can I do to get my dog to actually listen to me?" Well, that's a bit like asking what a person can do to get better gas mileage. Trust me; everybody and their uncle has an opinion on that one!

That being said, there is one thing I wish all dog owners would do. And if they would, I really think the majority of dog and owner problem behaviors would be solved. That's hand feeding!

The strategy is really pretty simple. It all goes back to the saying "Don't bite the hand that feeds you." When you hand feed your dog, you make yourself more important, you teach bite inhibition and you get your pooch to pay more attention -- all without being mean to your dog! Let's break this idea down into the three smaller pieces to get the whole picture.

First, hand feeding your dog makes you more important in your dog's eyes. Some trainers call this "being the pack leader." Others call it "being the alpha dog." I simply call it making yourself the most important or most necessary thing in your dog's life. To be honest, I don't put any credence in the idea of pack theory and I could care less who the "pack leader" is in my house!

I look at leadership with my dogs this way: if I control all the really important resources in Fido's world, then it becomes pretty apparent who is in charge. This is like playing hard to get . . . you won't get what you want until I get what I want. So, if you hand feed every piece of food to your dog for at least 30 days, Fido will very quickly understand that, without Mom or Dad, he might not get fed! This is a great way to bond with your dog and build a better relationship.

The second aspect of hand feeding is how it impacts bite inhibition. I believe all dogs need to be taught to be careful with their mouths and teeth when interacting with people. There is no better way to get this point across than hand feeding. It gives me the perfect opportunity to focus on giving pieces of kibble, one or two at a time, and to teach the command "gentle." Others will call it "easy" or "nice." I could care less what you call it as long as you are doing it!

If the dog touches your finger with teeth, I can say "ouch," with a calm voice or use the command "gentle" and withhold the food for, let's say

10-15 seconds, then repeat the process. Before you know it, the land shark you have been living with will become the polite and patient dog you wanted in the first place!

If you do it right, you will find that when you say "ouch," most dogs will actually begin licking you as a way to express their apology for getting too rough. Licking is an apology and appeasement behavior in dogs! So simply by feeding our dogs by hand, we are teaching them to have better mouth skills (bite inhibition) with humans, humans who they need for the stuff they want. But wait! There's more . . .

So hand feeding your dog is important and it helps to keep your dog paying attention. But why does that matter? Regardless of whether you are a dog or a person, we all tend to pay more attention to those in our life who dole out the rewards, paychecks or praise. Unfortunately, the opposite can be said for those who punish, yell or take things away -- we avoid those folks like the plague! By simply looking at the relationship between you and your dog, and determining who controls those resources, you can put yourself right at the top of Fido's list of people he needs to survive in this big old world! You're being a leader without having to resort to being a butt-head!

I hope as you are reading this you are taking inventory of all the resources your pooch has and how you can use them in training, and in everyday life as well. There is a very simple mistake many people make when trying to control resources with a dog, and that's the idea that control is negative in some way. Think of it like this: spoiling a dog or child is thought to be a bad thing, but what if the spoiling only occurs when the dog or child has earned it? Would we consider that bad? The ultimate goal is to be necessary in your dog's life, not to control that life! So get out there and hand feed your pooch and see the difference it will make!

Are you ready for step two? Flip the page and keep reading . . .

Sit Say Please

Have you ever wished your dog could say please? Wouldn't this be an awesome way for our dogs to show their manners? Imagine having a command that required your dog not only to ask for something, but also to show the proper energy level when asking, before receiving permission to get or do something!

Sit is something every dog does, but we rarely take advantage of that behavior. We should be using it for more than a simple obedience command. I'm not talking about a Sit with Fido's body vibrating or his tail dusting the floor, basically out of control. I'm talking about a Sit where the dog is focused on you and what you are offering. Sit is usually the first thing we ask our dog to learn, but we rarely use it to achieve anything else. So, how can we use this basic command to teach our dogs manners?

Simple! From this point forward, we are going to use Sit as a way for our dogs to say "please."

This command will become a condition for our dog to receive the things he wants. Plus, he will have to wait until we give permission to get what he wants. Sit will now be used for specific reasons. For example, use Sit to identify who controls the food, where Fido sleeps, where he is allowed to be and how he asks for things!

Until now, we have pleaded, cried, and even screamed at our dogs to get what we wanted. Some people even resort to manhandling their dogs to get a behavior. As many have figured out, forcing a dog to do something the dog doesn't want to do rarely yields a positive outcome. Why not try getting our dog to present proper manners and appropriate energy to get what he wants? Remember, dogs don't get anything for free! In addition to giving us that wanted behavior, the dog must also present an appropriate energy level. Simply put, Fido must Sit and "say please" with the proper energy level before he gets anything!

Unlike many trainers, I don't like to use Sit as my primary stay or duration command. I find that when a dog is asked to sit or stay for longer than 30 seconds, many simply get bored and lay down – can't say I blame them! I tend to use Down for duration stays and Sit for "Please" or "Paying Attention." Why use Sit for Please? It's all about leadership!

You need to be seen as the leader in your home. And leadership with dogs is created through resource control, not some of the crap – excuse my choice of words – you have either read, seen on TV or been told. Resource control does not necessitate scruff shakes, alpha rolls, pinning down or staring down your dog. What resource control means is that before your dog goes outside, gets food, gets their leash put on, gets attention or love, or even hops up on the couch with you, that dog must SIT, with the correct energy, and say please!

To walk you through how it works, let's take a look at feeding time in the Deathe household. Let's start with a question: if I leave food out all the time and do not require the dog to work for his or her meal, who owns or controls that food resource? Yep, you got it: the dog! This is not an issue for all dog owners, but if there is confusion over who owns the food resource, snippy and snarky behavior around their food or food bowls can result!

So what do we do? I ask my dogs to SIT before I place the bowl on the ground. After setting it down, I cue the dog to wait and then release the dog to eat his meal. Fido has worked for his meal and has shown the proper energy level needed to be released to receive it. If feeding time is done correctly, your dog makes the connection that you control the food resource in this family, not him. As time goes by, you will notice that Fido will offer this "please" (Sit) command without being asked. This is basic psychology. The cue becomes conditioned as a way for the dog to get the desired response. We get the manners and the dog gets the reward.

I even took this one step further with my sons, having Donovan and Dylan do the daily feeding with the dogs. I do this because I feel the food resource is the easiest thing for a child to control. Let me be clear: at no time do I recommend a child be left alone with dogs! I oversee the process, while my sons actually do the feeding. It is a great way for me to bond with my kids and it's also a great way my sons to bond with the dogs. This is just one example of using Sit to control manners and energy levels. Here are some other times saying "Please" can be used.

- **Getting the leash put on**
- **Going in and out a door**
- **Saying hello to another dog or person**
- **Being allowed on a couch or bed**
- **Getting petted/loved**

I am sure that as you begin this technique, you will continue to find everyday examples of how this can help you keep the family unit in the right order. Keep it up and don't give in to your dog.

Otherwise, you might have to ask yourself who is training who!

Non-Negotiable Rules

Over the course of my private sessions and my group training classes, many have heard me refer to the "non-negotiable rules" when it comes to human and dog relationships. It occurred to me that while I might give examples (like requiring a Sit as a please) and I even talk about them in my classes, I have never really defined what these non-negotiable rules are and why I stress using them so much. So let's not waste any time . . .

Non-negotiable rules are the behaviors you expect your dog to exhibit every day. These behaviors not only instill good manners, but these behaviors put you -- the human -- in a role of leadership. These rules also give us the opportunity to work with our dog, without carving out "training" time each day. Instead you just live your life as normal and you and Fido simply go through the day based on the rules you have chosen. Without even realizing it, Fido is trained just by interacting with his human every day . . .

These rules are also crucial in gaining impulse control! From where I stand, it is really the lack of impulse control which causes most problem behaviors. Think about it: Fido wants something, he goes for it and frustration ensues. Fido is living his life based on what he wants, rather than what it is that will make his human happy. How much better would life be if we could get Fido to stop and think before acting?

So, the big question: just what rules should you require?

That is an answer you as the "owner" have to decide! Your trainer (hint, hint -- if you don't have one and are reading this book, you probably should) can give you suggestions on achieving the goals you have for Fido. But in the end, you have to decide what behaviors are wanted and unwanted. The fact is, what I want from my dogs might be totally different than what you want from your dog! This is the main reason I refer to myself as a Pet Dog Trainer rather than obedience trainer. My job is to help people successfully live with their pet dog based on what the people want and need!

As you are thinking of your rules, let me share my top 10 non-negotiable rules, things I require of my dogs each day. These things improve my dogs' behavior and keep me in the role of "Top

Dog" without having to resort to being a "Butt-Head" to my dogs.

These are my Non Negotiable Rules:
1. *Sit and/or Down at every door*
2. *Sit and/or Down before every meal*
3. *Sit before leash is put on*
4. *Ask permission before getting on furniture or beds. This means a Sit, then being invited up (you make the final choice).*
5. *Walks only continue if there is no pulling. Fido pulls? The walk stops until he calms down and sits. Then, we will try again.*
6. *Go to crate on command using "go to bed" or "kennel up."*
7. *Crazy behavior equals no attention. If the dog gives any unwanted behavior, I ignore for one to two minutes.*
8. *Dog must have a reliable "leave it" command. Dog should know that "leave it" means "move back and wait for further instructions."*
9. *Dog must have reliable recall or consistently come when called. This should work in the house, outside, at the park and, yes, even at the dog park.*
10. *Dog must stay behind you on stairs, with the "wait" command. This should be used at doors as well. Dog knows to stay behind you until invited to move forward. "Excuse me" or "Back up"*

is the other side of this coin, where the dog understands to get out of the way for you to move through.

So your next job is simple: you have to call a family meeting, get everyone around the kitchen table and decide what your non-negotiable rules will to be. Take as many of mine as you like. If you think four of mine are dumb, that's cool! Just pick new ones that fit your life. After all, these are your rules, not mine.

Be careful not to overdo it, though. I recommend picking only 10 rules. Any more rules and you won't remember them all. Any less than 10 and you won't see the benefit of living life with them.

A final thought about this family pow wow on Non-Negotiable Rules: if everyone in the family is not on board with all the rules, then you are wasting your time. These need to be rules everyone agrees on, rules everyone will take the time to enforce. As always, Keep it Simple Stupid! In the end, families find it hard to "make the time" or "be consistent" when it comes to training their dogs! Creating your own list of non-negotiable rules and sticking to them fixes both issues.

I'm sure you are aware of the idea in dog training that we must "rule over," "be the boss," or in some cases even dominate the dog to achieve and keep a leadership role. In my opinion, this is not necessary and just plain mean in many case. Leadership, whether with dogs or people, is all about resource control!

If I control the dog's most important resources; food, water, access to my attention or even access to other things he enjoys (like furniture, beds, toys and so on), I will naturally become the leader without having to resort to physical force. This is as simple as relying on your brain instead of your brute! So get out paper and a pencil and come up with your own list of non-negotiable rules. Start using them and, in no time, you and Fido will be on your way to living a happy, healthy and relaxed life together!

Problem Behaviors and The 15 Minute Ignore

We have our rules. We ask for the dog to say please. We even feed the dog by hand! But what do we do when Fido does something wrong? Let's say, for instance, Fido jumps all over us when we get home? Well, the answer is what I call a 15 minute ignore.

There is one surefire way to fix many bad behaviors: ignore the bad behavior! I don't care how hard it might seem. You will not talk to, look at or address the dog in any way while the bad behavior is happening! Sounds simple, I know, but just keep reading . . .

Look at this technique in action when coming home to a crazy dog. You will start by walking in and not looking at the dog. If Fido jumps up on you, you will not touch the dog. Rather, you will turn your back on the dog or, preferably, you will walk right by. Some dogs are over the top and will jump up on your back. In this case, you may have to leave the room, shut the door or even temporarily use a baby gate to separate you and the dog. The fact is, the jumping behavior earns Fido nothing!

- *A word of caution here . . . If you are dealing with a puppy and are potty training at this point as well, then the ignoring must come after letting the dog out to go potty. I don't want folks mad at me, saying, "I ignored my dog and Fido peed on the carpet!" Instead, still ignore the bad behavior of jumping and quietly get the dog outside. Truly begin the "15 minute Ignore" after the dog has gone potty! Back to our regularly scheduled topic . . .*

Go in the kitchen and make yourself a glass of iced tea (or maybe an adult beverage -- age consenting, of course!). If the behavior continues, go into the bedroom and change clothes, and shut the door if necessary. The goal here is that until you get the behavior you want -- that's a dog who is not jumping on you -- you will not respond. By ignoring the behavior, you withhold the reward of your attention. This is where many owners fail. Read on and I will explain how to start training your dog using the 15 minute ignore, rather than Fido training you!

The entire objective of the 15 minute ignore is to take back leadership in your own house! Hopefully, I have convinced you that in many cases your dog has learned how to push your buttons and get exactly what he wants from his favorite human. Don't feel bad -- my ex-wife points out to me on a regular basis that if I can see this in my dogs, then why do I let my kids rope me into this scenario daily? So, you let dogs push your buttons and I let my 10 and 13 year old boys push mine! That should at least make you feel better. The end result is the same -- we allow ourselves to forget the golden rule of **ignore the bad and reward the good**. I simply ask for 15 minutes max and we should be able to fix both the dogs and the kids!

Let's think about kids when they are young. We go through the grocery store and do everything we can to avoid the candy aisle. But we take one wrong turn and there we are. Our kids start asking for candy and we tell them no. Then our kids start yelling and screaming that they want the candy and throw a fit right there in the store. Haven't we all been there at one time or another? We are mortified as people start to stare.

Here is the turning point . . . we can give in, just to stop the embarrassment, and give them the candy. We can pick them up or take their hands and leave the store without finishing the shopping. Or we can ignore the behavior, continue down the aisle and complete the shopping, without reacting at all to the temper tantrum. That was my Mom's favorite technique . . .

We are back to not touching, talking or addressing the dog; in essence, you need to ignore them. Be ready, though. Fido is not used to this insolence from his human. He will try every trick in the book to get you to flinch -- much like your children. Do not blink. Most dogs don't even make it 15 minutes. At the 8-9 minute mark, they get all pissy and say "To hell with you!" and sulk off in the corner. They lay down with that huffing noise that only a disgruntled dog can make.

Be careful and don't get cocky, because you are only halfway there. You must now wait a few minutes and allow the dog to remain in that relaxed state. This is the moment you have been waiting for. Now, reward the dog for the good job he did being calm! Call the dog to you and lavish him with love. If you can pull this off for let's say, 4-5 weeks, you will have a dog who will not jump up on you when you walk in the door, because that behavior gets them nothing positive! Fido now realizes if he wants Mom or Dad's attention, being calm will get him what he wants.

Now if your dog is already comfortable with the sit command and is regularly using sit to get what they want (remember **Sit - Say Please**?), you may have something to incorporate into the 15 minute ignore, sitting down. If, after you have ignored the jumping up behavior, Fido comes to you and sits on his own, you need to take advantage of this and reward that behavior. This means he has figured out that rather than behaving inappropriately, if he sits at your side, that is a suitable behavior rather than jumping up, so he gets your attention. Take advantage of this and lavish him with even more love. As time progresses, Fido will begin to use sit, or he'll go lay down sooner upon your entry into the house and there will be fewer instances of jumping up to greet you.

After all that, you can finally answer the question of who is training who -- and you can answer it the right way! Remember: Keep It Simple Stupid! Ignore the bad and reward the good. Or, if you're really smart, redirect the bad and reward an even better behavior!

Exercise: Reality Vs. Myth

So here we are, at Step Five. Honestly, this one has very little to do with resource control. But it has helped many of my clients through the tough times of a crazy and energetic dog, so cut me some slack on deviating from my theme and keep reading.

Every hydraulic system has a set pressure it can withstand. Go over that allowed pressure, or exceed critical mass? Well, boom! You can look at Fido's behavior in the same way. Each behavior has its own pressure tank. That includes barking, digging, jumping, play biting and, yes, even pulling on a leash! If we are smart owners and keep the pressure under critical mass, the behaviors remain normal. Problems never surface and life is good! But if we allow the pressure to build? You probably already know what happens. And you may be experiencing that, or you would not be reading this book!

If your dog pulls like a demon, you have allowed that tank to overflow. Consequently, you probably hate walking Fido! What you have not considered is that once the walking tank overfills, that pressure has to go somewhere else. Now, you not only have a leash issue, but Fido has started barking at everything. As the barking tank overflows, Fido might start digging to China in your backyard. And so the story goes until I, the dog trainer, receive a phone call from a prospective client telling me how the dog is completely out of control!

But the simple translation is a dog whose pressure capacity has been taxed to the point of complete hydraulic failure! At this point, take a deep breath. Realize this now out-of-control behavior actually started with just one behavior and the only way to fix this, is to fix the behaviors the same way they occurred: one at a time.

The key to a happy, healthy and well-behaved dog is simple: exercise! This is the channel we rarely consider for our out-of-control and over-pressured hydraulic systems! The only way to fix the leak is to first lower the pressure in the system – that's exercise – and then re-train the system! So, what is energy in regards to a dog, and just how do we exercise or vent the system? While it might sound simple, all dogs are different. That means energy types and requirements are as different as the dogs in question!

Take, for example, a Golden Retriever. Golden Retrievers have been bred for retrieving, so their energy type is generally running and fetching things. In comparison, a schnauzer, bred as a varmint hunter, has energy geared to tracking small moving critters, and they really like to bark! Beagles are similar in that they love to bark, but they use their nose instead of tracking the moving objects. What about a Husky or a Malamute? They were bred to pull sleds (and everything else attached to them). An Australian Shepherd's goal in life is to herd things. Now, consider the classic – and my favorite! – the mutt. Mutts might have parts of some, if not all, of these dog energy types! Needless to say, you had better be willing to do some homework on your dog and really find out what trips their trigger!

To many dog owners, the backyard, a 15 minute walk (really only an excuse to pee!) or two days a week in "doggy day care" are foolishly considered enough mental and physical exercise for that four-legged best friend!

_ There are two myths in dog training. Let's bust those bubbles now before we go any further . . . _

* _ Myth 1: My dog has a big backyard and gets plenty of exercise. The backyard is not exercise,

period. It's more like your office. When you were first awarded or promoted to your new office, it was awesome. You could not wait to decorate with family pictures, diplomas and, of course, a new pencil cup and desk calendar from the office supply superstore. For at least the first three or four months, your office was the most stimulating environment on earth! Now, ask yourself: how stimulating is your office? Yep, you will do anything to get out and just do something different, right? Well, that should help to understand why the grass is always greener on the other side – or why your dog has become destructive or started escaping from your backyard! Trust me, folks: backyards are not exercise. If overused, they actually become frustration boxes._ *

- _ Myth 2: The walk. Look, walking your dog is a great leadership and bonding exercise. It teaches the dog to walk with us, not against us. And it gives you both something to do together. But in reality, unless you are a runner or walking your dog two or three hours a day, one walk does not really wear out a dog. In most cases, dogs across America are lucky to get 20-30 minute walks. You and I both know that just ain't gonna cut it!_ *

As a dog trainer and volunteer in animal shelters, I stress that people must think before they get a dog as a pet! If your lifestyle is one in which hour-long walks, trips to the dog park, classes in agility, rally or scent work (let alone basic obedience) are not achievable, don't get a dog! Dogs actually require work! There is no law saying every family is required or even ought to own a dog. Okay, off my soapbox and back to exercise.

Exercise needs to be both mental and physical! Dogs cannot live off bread (exercise) alone. They need some variety! Simply walking your dog daily won't cut it. You might need to add agility or rally obedience work to exercise your dog's mind too. This might even require finding a herding class to allow your dog's more primal needs to come to the surface! If, as an owner, you are unable to exercise your dog one week, consider adding three days a week of doggy day care, which will also help with socialization! There is no one "magic bullet."

So what do you do now? I cannot believe I am saying this, but calling a dog trainer is probably not your first step! Take a serious look in the mirror and ask yourself: am I giving my dog all the exercise and mental stimulation needed to make him happy and balanced? I would guess that, if you are honest, the answer is no. And your first step to fixing the problem is staring back at you in the mirror – it's you! Before calling a trainer to prescribe a "magic" dog training pill, get out and start living life with your dog and help Fido! Just be with and spend time with your dog! If you are lucky, you just might solve your "problem behaviors" without having to call a dog trainer!

What's next? Well, you might need to call that trainer with step two, to help with the retraining and finding better outlets for the behavior which will allow for a higher pressure limit in your dog's hydraulic system! But calling a trainer before you actually take time to exercise your dog is futile and expensive. What we (the dog trainers) will do is charge you hard-earned money to tell you to walk your dog more, take Fido to a dog park, enroll Fido in a fun competition-style class or challenge your dog's mind with interactive toys or games. Doesn't that sound just like what I shared with you in the above paragraphs, and for free?

So why, you ask, is this exercise piece so important? Without cutting the edge (decreasing pressure) from the dog first, formal training or obedience will be essentially impossible!

Like kids, there is no magic pill or silver bullet when working with dogs. There is only time and effort! You and your dog will bond better, love more and be better friends the sooner we get everyone on board with this idea! I leave you with two thoughts to chew on...

_ 1.   **A Tired Dog Is A Good Dog!** _

_ 2. **Nothing good ever comes from less, only from more!** _

Will This Stuff Really Work?

Okay, so you have reached the end . . . I really hope you enjoyed the book and you've learned at least a few things to help you and your pooch get back on the same page. As I said earlier, I've been covering these ideas with my clients and I've seen how much these techniques helped, and that's the reason I wrote this book. Let's face it -- many folks cannot afford the price of a good in-home trainer to help with their dog! So I hope this book finds its way into the hands of those folks.

These ideas are not complicated, and these ideas fit right into my world of Keep it Simple Stupid . . . I promise if you are consistently frequent (one of my favorite sayings!) with the ideas you found in this book, you will, in the end, have the Perfect Pet Dog!

As always, thanks for the support and the purchase of this book. If you enjoyed it, please give us a review on your favorite online book store, so we can make it even easier for folks to find these solutions for them and their dogs!

If you're interested in having me talk to your dog group, club or any other group that would enjoy this kind of discussion, please contact me through our website: www.kissdogtraining.com. You can get all sorts of other cool, free info from our blog or social media pages! All those links are available on the website.

Good luck with your pooch -- and remember to Keep it Simple Stupid!

Mike

www.ingramcontent.com/pod-product-compliance
Lightning Source LLC
Chambersburg PA
CBHW052119070526
44584CB00017B/2554